For all children who love animals
and especially for Jonathan, Aria, Peter and Brendan

How the Sun Was Made

An Aboriginal Legend
Retold and illustrated by
Katherine Morris

Little Hills Press

Long ago,
in the darkness of early dreamtime,
only birds and animals
lived in Australia.

The good Spirit who lived up in the sky
watched over the world below.

In those far off days
there was no sun.
The only light came
from the moon and stars.

Of all the birds
Brolga was the most graceful.

She would often dance,
stepping and bowing,
stretching and turning.

Sometimes, when the moon
shone high and full in the sky,
Brolga would even
spread her wings and fly.

Although Emu was the biggest
bird of all she was jealous
of Brolga.

"Why can't I dance like Brolga?"
grumbled Emu.
"Why can't I fly?"

But Emu was big and heavy.
Her wings were short.
She could not dance like Brolga
and she could not fly at all.

Emu became so jealous
that she began to quarrel with Brolga.

Nesting time came
and Emu laid her eggs
in a nest on the ground.

"Anyway, my chicks will be better
than yours!" snapped Emu
as Brolga passed by.

"Of course they won't!"
jeered Brolga.

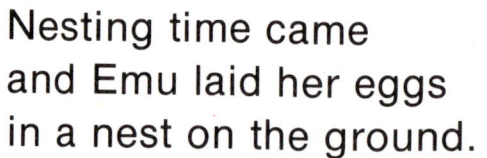

Emu sprang up
and began to fight with Brolga.

Brolga managed to escape from Emu.
Angrily, she seized one of Emu's eggs
and sent it spinning
high into the sky
where the Good Spirit
had gathered a great heap
of wood.

Instead of falling back to earth
the emu egg went speeding upwards.

Higher and higher it soared,
nearer and nearer
to the great pile of wood.

Crash!

The shell shattered!
The yellow yolk broke
and burst into flames.

Sticks and wood caught alight
and a brilliant fire
lit up the sky.

The sun was shining
for the first time.

As the sun's rays
reached the earth,
colours glowed,
flowers sparkled
and the world
was filled with light.

Birds flew happily around
and animals gazed in wonder
as the very first day began.

Like a red-gold ball
the sun-fire shone in the sky
lighting up the earth below.

Kookaburra was so happy
that he began to laugh.

Kookaburra's laughter
echoed through the bushland
until even the Good Spirit
up in the sky
could hear the merry sound.

The Good Spirit
looked down with delight.
"How beautiful the earth looks now!"
he thought.

During the day
the sun-fire burned brightly.
Kookaburra and all the others
enjoyed the light and warmth
of the sun.

As the sun-fire died down
night came again to the earth
and the birds and animals went to sleep.

Then the Good Spirit gathered more wood
to light the sun-fire again.

A new day began.
The sun shone brightly on the earth
but most of the birds and animals
were still asleep.

Then the Good Spirit called to Kookaburra:
"If you will laugh every morning
when I light the sun-fire
your merry sound will let the others know
that day is about to begin."

Kookaburra chuckled.
"All right," he said.
"You light the sun-fire
and I shall laugh.
Between us we can
awaken the world."

And so they did!

When the sun-fire
lit up the sky again
birds and animals awoke
to the sound
of Kookaburra's laughter.

The quiet darkness of night
was followed by the wonder
and delight of each new day.

Kookaburra has kept his promise.

To this day you can hear him
laughing at sun-rise
just as he did in the dreamtime
so long ago.

Legends of Australian Aborigines explained the reason for many things they saw about them. This beautiful legend which tells how the sun was made and describes the coming of day also features some of Australia's best known birds.

KOOKABURRA

The kookaburra is a member of the kingfisher family. It is also, known as the Laughing Jackass because of its laughter which is heard most often at sunrise and sunset.

A family of kookaburras lives in its own territory in the open forest or woodland. Nests are made in hollows in trees. After the young kookaburras hatch they remain in the nest for about a month. Then for another two or three months food is brought to them. Older birds from a previous hatching also help to feed and care for the young.

Kookaburras feed on insects and small animals. They are famous for catching snakes which they drop from a height and thrash against the ground or a tree branch before eating.

BROLGA

The Brolga, sometimes called the Native Companion, is Australia's only true crane. It is noted for its beautiful dancing.

Brolgas live together in flocks on grassy plains, often by a swamp or lagoon. Their loud trumpeting cry can be heard from a great distance.

Many birds will dance together spreading their wings as they circle, leap and bow to one another. Their long wings enable the brolgas to fly easily at great heights.

Brolgas lay only two eggs on the ground or if near water on a grassy platform. Both the parent birds care for the chicks.